# ADVERTISING & MARKETING

**CLIVE GIFFORD**

Heinemann Library
Chicago, Illinois

© 2006 Heinemann Library
a division of Reed Elsevier Inc.
Chicago, Illinois

Customer Service 888–454–2279

Visit our website at www.heinemannlibrary.com

Photo research, design and illustration by Trocadero Publishing, An Electra Media Group Enterprise, Suite 204, 74 Pitt Street, Sydney, Australia
Printed and bound in Hong Kong and China by Wing King Tong

10 09 08 07 06
10 9 8 7 6 5 4 3 2 1

**Library of Congress Cataloging-in-Publication Data**

Gifford, Clive.
  Advertising & marketing : developing the marketplace / Clive Gifford.
     p. cm. -- (Influence and persuasion)
  Includes bibliographical references and index.
  ISBN 1-4034-7651-9 (library binding-hardcover)
  1. Advertising--Juvenile literature. 2. Advertising agencies--Juvenile literature. 3. Advertising and children--Juvenile literature. 4. Marketing--Juvenile literature. I. Title: Advertising and marketing. II. Title. III. Series.
  HF5829.G54 2006
  659.1--dc22
                              2005015146

**Acknowledgments**
The publishers would like to thank the following for permission to reproduce photographs: The Advertising Archive 7, 35; Airbus Industrie 45; Alamy/Patrick Eden 22 (bottom); Brand X Pictures 9, 10, 17, 18, 19, 20, 23 (top), 36, 37, 38, 39, 40, 41, 42, 43, 48, 49, 52, 55, 56, 57, 58; Comstock Images 22 (top), 51; Corbis/Reuters 13; Flat Earth Picture Gallery 47; Getty Images/Photodisc 44; Kobal/MGM/Eon 29; Newspix/Chris Crerar 50; Newspix/ Michael Dodge 53; Oronsay Imagery/Scott Brodie 5, 6, 8, 11, 15, 25, 27; Oronsay Imagery 30; Popperfoto 32; State Library of NSW 33; US National Archives 12, 31

Cover photograph reproduced with permission of Alamy/Ian Shaw

# Contents

# Introduction

By the time you reach the age of eighteen, there is a good chance that you will have already watched thousands of TV commercials. That is just the start. Researchers estimate that a person moving through a busy town or city is bombarded by more than 3,000 different examples of advertising every day.

## What is advertising?

Everyone is familiar with the advertisements played during breaks in television or radio shows, and the glossy printed advertisements for toys, fashion, sportswear, and food in magazines. But advertising comes in dozens of forms, including billboards, direct mail, and banners and pop-up windows that appear on the Internet.

Advertising is a type of communication that tells you something by using words, pictures, music, or moving images. It is frequently designed to communicate to many people. Advertising posters and billboards on display at the 2004 Athens Olympics, for example, were seen by a total television audience of more than a billion people.

## Who are the advertisers?

An advertiser is a company or an individual who pays for advertising. The advertiser often uses a company called an advertising agency to help them prepare a campaign and communicate their message to their target audience – the people the advertiser most wants to reach.

Influencing and convincing a target audience to adopt an idea or take a particular action is advertising's primary goal. The advertiser often wants people to buy their product or service. At other times, the advertiser wants people to think more highly of the company or organization that has placed the ad. Some advertising seeks to change people's views on issues or to convince them to vote a certain way in an election.

# Why Use Advertising?

Less than 200 years ago, companies spent little or no money on advertising. Today, the largest companies spend hundreds of millions of dollars every single year. Why? In a word, power. Advertising has the power to influence and persuade people to adopt certain ideas or beliefs, or perform a wide range of actions, from donating to a charity to changing the way they live.

Advertising grew out of the need for companies to announce their products in order to sell them to the public. Some advertising, such as classified ads in newspapers or direct mail campaigns that include order forms in letters sent to potential customers, tries to sell direct to customers. Most

## Push to smell

In 2003, some Londoners waiting for buses at bus stops were encouraged by ads to use their sense of smell. A button could be pushed that released a sample of the new scent of Head and Shoulders shampoo.

advertising, though, is only one part – although an important one – of the entire process of influencing potential customers and selling to them.

Without advertising, it is almost impossible for companies to launch a new product and get it known well enough for sales to make a profit. Advertising, if performed well and placed in the right media channels at the right time, can create an awareness of a product in thousands, or even millions, of people. Advertising can also generate an interest in the product and, sometimes, a desire to own it.

Much advertising spending is targeted older products rather than new ones. Companies fight hard to increase or keep their share of the market for a product, especially household goods such as food and soaps that are bought frequently. Some ads may be targeted at people using rival brands, encouraging them to switch with trial offers and competitions. Other campaigns may be designed to reassure those who have already bought a product and urge them to continue doing so. Further campaigns may seek to remind people of the value or benefits of a product to keep it in mind the next time they go shopping.

## Chewing gum success

More than a dozen chewing gum companies existed in the United States when William Wrigley Jr. arrived in Chicago in 1891 with just $32 in his pocket. However, by using extensive advertising in magazines, newspapers, and billboards, Wrigley's became and remains the leading brand in the United States, with nearly half the share of a market worth almost $2 billion a year.

" Advertising is the most potent influence in adapting and changing the habits and modes of life, affecting what we eat, what we wear, and the work and play of the whole nation."

Calvin Coolidge,
president of the United States,
1923–1929

Advertising can also promote new uses or new ways of using an old product. In the United States, Canada, and the United Kingdom, for instance, advertising has been used to persuade consumers to make turkey part of meals throughout the year, not just on occasions such as Thanksgiving or Christmas. Products can also be given a makeover and repositioned in a market. Volvo cars, for example, have long had a reputation for safety. But Volvo's recent advertising all over the world has been geared toward making the public think of Volvo vehicles as stylish and sporty as well as safe.

## Changing habits

Advertising is used not only to launch new and reinforce old products, but also to inform and

## Repositioning soft drinks

Early Coca-Cola advertising claimed the drink was close to being a medicine, with claims that it could "revive and sustain" as well as cure headaches. By the 1920s, the drink had been repositioned as a quality and fun refreshment.

A similar repositioning occurred with another soft drink during the 1980s. Lucozade, a drink popular in the United Kingdom, went from being a tonic for people feeling sick to a sports drink after a series of ads featuring Olympics sports stars.

attract new consumers. As people grow older, they become the target for different products. As teens grow up and get jobs, for example, they may require bank accounts and credit cards. As people enter old age, they may require certain health-related products.

Some products such as acne creams for teenagers and baby products for new mothers are only used by a particular group of consumers for a short period. Companies must advertise regularly in order to attract their next group of customers.

An advertiser often has more than one goal for its ad campaigns. It may try to keep its market share through

## Slogans

Slogans are short advertising phrases designed to be memorable. Over time, many of these enter the regular language. Nike's "Just Do It" and the DeBeers diamond company's "A diamond is forever" are two examples.

TV commercials. At the same time, it may target potential new users by advertising in suitable magazines and encouraging people to switch from another product by offering free trials or coupons in newspapers or through direct mail.

*Advertisers value the teenage market because they believe that brand loyalty developed at this time will continue throughout life.*

*Business today is all about relationship building. B2B advertising is a key to linking one business with another to their mutual benefit.*

## B2B and recruitment advertising

A significant portion of the advertising industry is devoted to advertising the goods and services of one business to another. This is known as Business To Business or B2B advertising. B2B advertising is often done through trade newspapers and magazines and at exhibitions and conferences for a particular industry. B2B advertisers tend to target their goods and services at a smaller number of potential buyers than consumer goods, but, if successful, the orders can be much larger in value.

Advertising is also used to recruit people as volunteers or employees. Recruitment advertising for individual jobs is a specialized branch of the advertising industry that tries to attract the "perfect" customer. Unlike campaigns for consumer goods like food or cars, the advertisements

### Corporate image

Corporate image advertising focuses on improving how a company and its work is seen by its target audience, such as other companies or the public.

Companies at work in the nuclear power industry, for example, advertise heavily in order to convey messages about reliability and strict safety levels to reassure the public.

*This sculpture, located outside the United Nations building in New York, aptly illustrates the goals of the Gun Control Network.*

## Changing laws

In 1997, members of the Gun Control Network – a lobby group that campaigns for tighter controls on guns of all kinds – parked a truck outside the Houses of Parliament in London. A debate was being held over the introduction of a law banning some guns but not .22-caliber handguns.

The truck carried a poster of famous U.S. politician Robert Kennedy, who was shot dead with a .22 handgun in 1968. The slogan on the poster read, "If a .22 handgun is less deadly, why isn't he less dead?" An amendment to ban .22 handguns was added to the bill.

must appear quickly. They are often placed on the Internet, in magazines and journals about that industry, or in national and local newspapers.

Governments and military forces have long used advertising for recruitment. At the start of World War I, for example, the British military launched an advertising poster campaign featuring an image of one of the country's most famous military leaders, General Kitchener, pointing straight out of the poster with the slogan, "Your Country Needs You." This helped recruit many volunteers to Great Britain's armed forces and was adapted by the U.S. army with a character named Uncle Sam.

During World War II, with many men away in military service, there was a serious shortage of workers in U.S. factories. Prompted and encouraged by government advertising, millions of women who had previously been housewives began working for the war effort. One of the most famous images from these ads was a painting of a strong and attractive woman at work, named Rosie the Riveter, who urged women to "Do The Job He Left Behind."

Today, governments are major advertisers. They publicize new laws and initiatives and encourage the public to know their rights and the benefits to which they are entitled.

## Wartime slogans

Advertising during wartime has been successful because it has managed to get the public to act in different ways in order to help the war effort. During World War II, for example, slogans such as "Careless Talk Costs Lives," a warning to look out for spies, and "Dig For Victory," which encouraged Britons to turn their gardens into food-growing land, were remembered and acted upon by thousands.

Many government campaigns in countries all over the world have been aimed at improving energy efficiency, preventing crime, and promoting a healthier lifestyle.

Some campaigns, such as discouraging people from drinking alcohol and driving, or encouraging them to install smoke detectors in their homes, or to be aware of the dangers of sunbathing because it can cause skin cancer, have been highly successful and have led to hundreds of thousands of people changing their behavior. In 2003, the U.S. government was one of the country's largest advertisers, spending only a few million dollars less than the McDonald's Corporation.

*An example of the Rosie the Riveter posters widely used by the U.S. government during World War II.*

Advertising is also used to influence and change people's beliefs or attitudes as well as their actions. Charities and lobby groups use advertising to highlight and explain issues and problems that face people, animals, or the environment. Through advertising, many issues, from land mines to sex equality in the workplace, have become subjects that are debated heavily in public.

Political parties in most countries make great use of advertising to get their messages across, but never more so than just prior to an election. Strict rules on how much can be spent on political advertising exist in many countries including the United Kingdom and Canada, but political spending on advertising can be very high in the United States, especially in an important election year. In 2000, political spending on TV advertising alone reached $672 million. In 2004, the figure was more than $1 billion.

## Where's the beef?

The phrase "where's the beef?" means that something lacks substance and content. It became a U.S.-wide catchphrase after being used as a slogan in an ad campaign for the Wendy's hamburger chain. During the 1984 presidential elections, Democratic presidential candidate Walter Mondale used it to criticize a rival because of his lack of clear policies.

# The Advertising Business

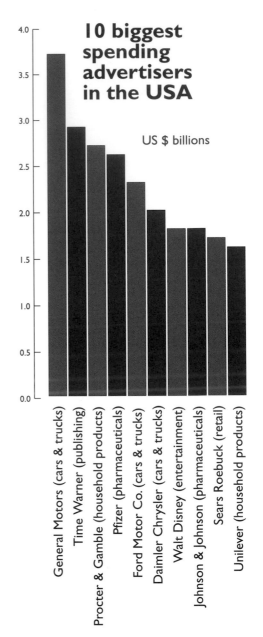

## 10 biggest spending advertisers in the USA

US $ billions

- General Motors (cars & trucks)
- Time Warner (publishing)
- Procter & Gamble (household products)
- Pfizer (pharmaceuticals)
- Ford Motor Co. (cars & trucks)
- Daimler Chrysler (cars & trucks)
- Walt Disney (entertainment)
- Johnson & Johnson (pharmaceuticals)
- Sears Roebuck (retail)
- Unilever (household products)

Despite economic difficulties in the first years of the 21st century, advertising remains a powerful and wealthy industry. Germany, Japan, and the United Kingdom are the world's second, third, and fourth largest advertising markets. In the United Kingdom in 2003, an estimated $30 billion was spent on advertising. This huge sum is just a fraction of the amount spent on advertising in the world's largest single market, the United States. In 2003, total spending on advertising in the United States exceeded $249 billion.

The advertising industry directly employs an estimated half a million people in the United States and many tens of thousands of people in other countries. This is only part of the picture. Many millions more depend on advertising for their livelihood. This is especially the case in media industries such as newspapers, and commercial radio and television, where advertising is frequently a company's main source of income. Advertisers spend large amounts of money to advertise. In the United States in 2003, more than $18 billion was spent on advertising on commercial radio.

## Big spenders

In 1881, U.S. company Procter & Gamble held a meeting to discuss how to advertise their floating soap, Ivory. Harley Procter, in charge of advertising at the company, asked, "Ivory is the finest soap we have ever made, but how are customers going to know about its virtues unless we tell them?" Reluctantly, the company increased its advertising budget from $1,500 to $11,000, a huge amount to spend on advertising at the time. As a result, Ivory became the number one soap brand in the United States. Today, after more than a century of high spending on advertising, Ivory remains one of the leading soap brands, but it is just a small part of the wide variety of goods sold by Procter & Gamble. According to *Advertising Age*, in 2002, Procter & Gamble spent $4.4 billion on advertising, more than any other company in the world. They were the third largest spender in the United States and the largest in Germany, China, and the United Kingdom.

*Through the power of advertising, a select number of global companies have become instantly recognizable anywhere in the world.*

## Project Blue

In 1996, PepsiCo launched a massive $500 million advertising campaign, known as Project Blue, to highlight its color change from red to blue and to renew its assault on Coke, the number one selling cola. From 1998 to 2001, Pepsi's sales grew by approximately 18 percent each year.

The advertising-to-sales ratio is one measure of how much is spent on advertising. This ratio shows what percentage of the total price of a product is made up of advertising. In the United States, for every dollar spent on soap, roughly 15 cents goes to advertising. In the entire food and drink industry, advertising averages roughly 10 percent (or 10 cents per dollar). In the United Kingdom, hair coloring products (34.5 cents per dollar), indigestion remedies (21.9 cents), denture cleaners (18.6 cents), and shampoos (18.4 cents) are the products with the highest advertising-to-sale ratios.

## Advertising agencies

Advertisers not only buy space and time in the media to place ads, they also spend heavily on hiring advertising agencies to research, prepare, launch, and monitor advertising campaigns. An estimated 42,000 companies in the United States work in advertising. A large number of these have fewer than 15 employees. At the other end of the scale are enormous international advertising agency networks, many of which have their headquarters in the United States.

## Top 10 global media spenders

| | Company | Headquarters | Industry | Annual spending $ millions |
|---|---|---|---|---|
| 1 | Procter & Gamble Co. | USA | Food, household products | 4479 |
| 2 | Unilever | UK/Netherlands | Food, household products | 3315 |
| 3 | General Motors | USA | Motor vehicles | 3218 |
| 4 | Toyota Motor Corp. | Japan | Motor vehicles | 2405 |
| 5 | Ford Motor Co. | USA | Motor vehicles | 2387 |
| 6 | Time Warner | USA | Media & communications | 2349 |
| 7 | Daimler Chrysler | Germany/USA | Motor vehicles | 1800 |
| 8 | L'Oreal | France | Cosmetics | 1683 |
| 9 | Nestle | Switzerland | Foodstuffs | 1547 |
| 10 | Sony Corp. | Japan | Electronic goods | 1513 |

Source: Advertising Age

## 10 largest advertising agencies worldwide, by revenue

| | Company | Headquarters | Revenue $ millions |
|---|---|---|---|
| 1 | Omnicom Group | New York | 7536.3 |
| 2 | Interpublic Group | New York | 6203.6 |
| 3 | WPP Group | London, UK | 5781.5 |
| 4 | Publicis Groupe | Levallois-Perret, France | 2711.9 |
| 5 | Dentsu | Tokyo, Japan | 2060.9 |
| 6 | Havas | Chicago | 1841.6 |
| 7 | Grey Global Group | New York | 1199.7 |
| 8 | Hakuhodo | New York | 860.8 |
| 9 | Cordiant Communications | Chicago | 788.5 |
| 10 | Asatsu-DK | Paris, France | 339.5 |

Source: *Advertising Age*

As early as 1899, U.S. advertising agency J. Walter Thompson opened an office in London, England, the first known foreign outpost for a U.S. advertising company. Many international agency networks have been created by companies being merged or taken over. For example, the fourth largest advertising network in the world, the Publicis Groupe, includes famous advertising agencies such as Saatchi & Saatchi and Leo Burnett Worldwide. In 2004, the Omnicom Group was the world's largest global agency. There are more than 30 individual agencies in its network.

*In many large cities around the world advertising agencies occupy large amounts of office space in specific business sectors. This leads other companies that offer support and services to the industry to find a home in these areas, such as in Los Angeles, shown here.*

*Advertising agencies are people businesses. Everything they do depends on the quality and creativity of their employees. This means there is a high level of co-operation between people to achieve the best result for a client.*

Advertising agencies compete hard for an advertiser's business, which is known as an account. While many accounts are small, accounts with major advertisers can be worth tens of millions. Unlike businesses such as food or clothing manufacturers that sell goods to hundreds of thousands of customers, ad agencies may only have a small number of clients, but they are clients that spend heavily. These clients may switch to another agency on short notice. Less than a quarter of all advertisers use the same ad agency for more than ten years.

## Success of the Saatchis

Nine years after leaving their original advertising company, Saatchi & Saatchi, Charles and Maurice Saatchi's latest advertising agency, M&C Saatchi, now makes a profit of $15 million a year. Selling shares on the UK stock market at the end of 2004 expected to net the two brothers $23 million each.

The fast-changing advertising scene puts enormous pressure on ad agencies, and especially on staff such as business managers whose job it is to bring in new accounts. It also places pressure on the staff who manage and handle current advertising accounts, and on the people who come up with the ads – the creative team. They need to deliver their very best work every single time.

Despite this pressure, advertising is considered a glamorous and exciting profession by many, and far more people want to get into the industry than there are jobs. There may be as many as 800 applications for a single job at some agencies.

With such competition, pay is often low to begin with, but there is the prospect of promotion or moving to a higher paid job as experience grows. Advertising agencies are only as good as the people they employ. T*he Economist* magazine estimates that almost two-thirds of an agency's income is spent on its staff.

At the very top, the rewards can be enormous. The top executives at large advertising agencies receive salaries measured in millions and bonuses worth as much as one-fifth of their annual salary.

*Jobs in the advertising industry are greatly sought after around the world, with as many as 800 applicants for each position.*

# Targets & Channels

entire population with their advertising and use all possible channels. So research must be done and decisions must be made about who to target for an ad campaign and what media channels to use in what ways.

During the 20th century, large amounts of research was done on how to distinguish people by occupation, wealth, age, and the region in which they live. This kind of analysis is known as demographics. Some demographic studies divide people into social groups or classes based on their occupation (see right). Much more research, in the form of market research and surveys, has taken place to find out what values, attitudes, and interests certain types and groups of people tend to share.

Advertisers and ad agencies face a large and bewildering array of different media, known as channels, in which they can advertise. They also have a massive potential audience, only part of which they most want to reach. The costs are simply too great for advertisers to target the

Companies that want to advertise and advertising agencies spend much time and effort defining their target audiences. A target audience is the group of consumers most likely to buy the product or service being advertised. Advertisers test their products on different focus groups of consumers and commission market research surveys. Companies may also use the services of market research bureaus. These exist in most countries and survey and track consumer groups. For a fee, they can provide statistics on different groups, their values, lifestyles, and what they consume, such as how many C1 men between the ages of 25 and 35 eat breakfast cereal, or what percentage of C2 housewives own cars.

At the end of their research, an advertiser may have a broad target audience such as "all males between the ages of 18 and 45" or a more narrow target audience such as "55- to 65-year-old A, B, and C1 women living on or near a large city."

# abcde
## Social class groupings

One system of grouping people by their occupation was known as the Registrar General's Social Scale in the UK and is now referred to as the ABC 1 scale in media and advertising.

**A** Higher managerial or professional

**B** Intermediate managerial and professional

**C1** Supervisory, clerical, and junior managerial and professional

**C2** Skilled manual

**D** Semi-skilled and unskilled manual

**E** Casual laborers, welfare recipients, and unemployed

Effective advertising, with the particular target audience clearly in mind, is then created and placed in the media.

## Advertising channels

Advertising media have developed rapidly. Where delivery trucks and bus stop shelters were unadorned in the past, they now tend to be covered in advertising. The same is the case with tickets for events, packaging for take-out foods, and credit cards. Each of these items, and many, many more, can carry advertising for completely different products and services.

The major advertising media for many years have been the press (newspapers and magazines), television, direct mail, radio, business directories such as the

*The Internet is a very important marketing channel for many businesses.*

Yellow Pages, the movies, and outdoor advertising. The Internet has recently been added to this list. Companies have exploited the popularity of the World Wide Web by building their own websites that feature product announcements and catalogs, contests and online ordering. They run banner ads on other websites that direct potential customers to their site. E-mail is also used to send targeted advertisements to people who may have signed up for a service, have registered their warranty online, or have shown an interest in receiving news from a company.

*A telephone interviewer will conduct market research for a major market research company.*

## Spam

When e-mail advertisements are sent to people without their consent, they are known as spam. Spam clutters up email accounts – in 2005, the U.S. Federal Trade Commission estimated that 60 percent of all email messages sent in the United States were spam.

## Surveying consumers

Approximately 72 million Americans every year are interviewed in opinion and marketing research studies and surveys.

*Sponsorship is a form of advertising that works well for a wide range of products. The advantage is that it is seen by many people in many different locations.*

## Top 8 US media channels, by advertising spending

### Total spending US$202 billion

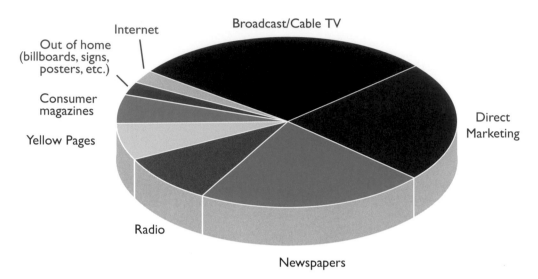

Source: *Advertising Age Factpack* 2004
(which itself cites: From Robert J. Coen's Universal
McCann U.S. Volume Report (AA, May 13, 2002),
The table shows all U.S. expenditures by all advertisers.)

Much of the spam advertises pornographic websites, prescription drugs, and sexual goods, but these messages are sent indiscriminately to email addresses, many of which are owned by children. Some PC software exists that can block spam, but much of it still reaches its target.

Different channels of the media tend to be used by different types of target audiences. For example, a business newspaper such as the *Wall Street Journal* or *The Financial Times* is likely to have far more A and B readers than any other social group.

Similarly, under 25s in many countries are more likely to listen to the radio or surf the Internet for news than read newspapers.

Target audiences rarely overlap perfectly with the available media channels, so advertisers have to plan and place campaigns over a range of different channels. They pay great attention to newspaper or magazine circulation, and TV and radio ratings, in order to determine how large the audience for their ads may be.

*A popular method used by advertisers is to attract attention and brand recognition through spectacular outdoor advertising.*

## Growth in US advertising spending, by media from 1990 to 2003

$ millions

Source:
U.S. Census Bureau, Statistical Abstract of the United States, 2004-2005

■ 1990
■ 2003

Chart categories (x-axis): Direct Mail, Newspapers, Television, Radio, Yellow pages, Magazines, Internet

y-axis: 0, 10000, 20000, 30000, 40000, 50000

## The power of television

Television is seen as one of the most effective means of advertising. It can reach millions of people and allows moving images to tell a story, demonstrate a product clearly, create a scene, or make a powerful statement. TV ads are usually watched at home as people relax and are more receptive to advertising messages. Television scheduling also allows advertisers to place their ads in or around the programs that their research shows are watched by the largest number of their target audience.

But television, like all media channels, has weaknesses. Viewers often use commercial breaks as a time to leave the room, and advanced digital TV recorders can record a show but edit out the ads. Most of all, television advertising is costly. Filming and producing an ad can easily cost $200,000. This is before time slots in commercial breaks have been paid for. Time slots vary greatly in price, based on the day and time of the week, and the ratings or audience for the TV program being shown.

In radio advertising, the "drive time" period when most people are in their cars, commuting to and from work, is usually the most expensive. Television's most expensive time slot comes during the National Football League's Super Bowl.

## TV audience research

Nielsen Media Research provides independent research on TV audiences' viewing habits to advertisers. It has installed over 5,000 devices called people-meters in U.S. homes. These track what channels are being watched at what times, and how many people are in the room. Nielsen backs this with a four-times-a-year TV diary sent to 2.5 million viewers, asking them to record their viewing habits for one week.

Watched by a national audience of an estimated 135 million Americans, a 30-second time slot at halftime can cost more than $2.4 million.

Sometimes, the line is blurred between advertising and the regular programming or editorial of the media channel in which the advertising appears. For example, advertorials are often found in local and national newspapers. They look a lot like the usual editorial pages and contain news and features, but they are actually a substantial advertisement paid for by an advertiser. In video games, TV shows, and movies, product placement can occur. This is where an advertiser pays to place their product or mentions of the product or its slogan in a prominent location in a movie, video game, or TV show.

*The James Bond film,* Die Another Day, *featured more product placement than any other major film before it. Twenty companies, including Revlon, Philips, Omega, and 7-Up paid a total of $70 million to place their products in the film. Aston Martin cars, such as the one seen here, have been featured in most of the Bond films since the 1960s. BMWs have also been used.*

# Advertising History

Advertising has a long history. Signs carved or painted into walls of Ancient Roman buildings, roughly 2,000 years ago, advertised taverns and rooms for rent. Town criers in Europe and Asia in medieval times would wander the streets shouting out simple advertising messages. However, the most common form of advertising was always simply one person mentioning something to another, a habit known as word of mouth.

In the 16th and 17th centuries, the use of the printing press began to spread across Europe. With paper scarce and expensive, the first ads were in small type, much like today's classified newspaper ads. Single-page advertising handbills, followed by newspapers, began to appear in Germany and Scandinavia, before spreading to the United Kingdom, North America, and elsewhere.

## Store front signs & symbols

Simple signs and symbols depicting what work goes on inside a building can be traced back to the Ancient Babylonians, more than 3,000 years ago. Some symbols found today, such as the three balls for a pawnbroker, or a red-and-white striped barber's pole, were first used more than 500 years ago.

## General Magazine

The first U.S. magazine to feature advertisements, the *General Magazine*, was published in 1742 by the inventor and statesman Benjamin Franklin.

The first newspapers only sold in small numbers to the wealthy, but great changes in the way people worked and lived were on their way. The Industrial Revolution introduced factories and machinery capable of making large quantities of goods. People started to move from the countryside into towns and cities to find work, more people learned to read, and newspapers were printed in greater numbers. In the United Kingdom, a very heavy tax on newspapers was partly lifted in 1833 and completely removed by 1855. Cheaper "penny papers" appeared that needed to sell large numbers and attract advertisers to make a profit. There was a massive boom in magazines and journals in the United States – by 1890, there were over 4,400 of them, selling eighteen million copies.

As the numbers of publications increased, the competition to sell space for ads on pages became intense. The first advertising agents began to appear in the early 19th century and were mainly employed by newspapers and magazines to sell space in the publications. Over time, advertising agents became independent agencies and started to both buy space in publications for customers and create and produce the ads on their customers' behalf.

During the 19th century, advertising developed more quickly in the United States than in any other country. Many Americans lived in isolated settlements far away from the stores of large towns. Companies first started to sell seeds and other farm equipment using printed catalogs sent in the mail. By the 1890s, thousands of items could be bought via mail order. Many people lived long distances away from doctors or pharmacists, and patent medicines that offered cures for every problem imaginable became very popular.

## Early advertising agency

One of the first known independent advertising agencies was formed in London in 1812. Reynell & Son, by the 1860s and 1870s, was offering creative advice and employing people to write ads and artists to provide illustrations.

## Kellogg's Corn Flakes

William Keith Kellogg placed his first advertisements for Corn Flakes in six local U.S. newspapers in 1906. Orders flooded in so quickly that Kellogg ran "apology ads" that urged customers to "stop buying, and give your neighbor a chance." These sparked even more demand, and by 1915, Kellogg was selling vast quantities of Corn Flakes and spending $1 million a year on advertising.

By 1893, there were approximately 110 companies in the United States spending more than $50,000 on advertising every year. Over half of these were patent medicine-makers.

Up until the 1870s, most household items, such as candles and food, were sold from unnamed bulk packages. Businesses started to produce packaged goods in their own factories and these carried company or brand names. Advertising was needed in order to sell the goods directly to customers. Among the early pioneers of branded goods, those that used advertising best survived and flourished. Breakfast cereal-makers, such as the American Cereal Co. that launched Quaker Oats – the first mass-produced cereal – became household names, as did a number of soap and cosmetics makers.

In the UK, Pear's Soap launched the slogan, "Good Morning! Have You Used Pear's Soap?" that linked an everyday phrase with their product. They imported 250,000 French coins

*By the 1950s supermarkets had begun to make a big difference in the advertising and marketing of food, with many new brands and variations of old brands becoming available.*

and had "Pears" stamped on them before giving them out to the public. This created enormous publicity, as did the buying of a famous painting to advertise their soap, and their annual Miss Pears competition, in which the best-looking young entrant had her portrait painted by a well-known artist.

## Rise of a giant

One of the earliest advertising agencies in the United States was founded in 1864. Called Carlton & Smith, it hired a young bookkeeper named James Walter Thompson. Ten years later, Thompson bought the agency from his bosses and re-named it after himself. Thompson paid more for the furniture in the company's office ($800) than for the business itself ($500). By 1890, it would be the first advertising agency to have clients bringing in more than $1 million a year. J. Walter Thompson introduced many innovations in advertising. It was one of the first advertising agencies to use high-quality photography in ads, and invented the job of account executive to take care of the advertising accounts of particularly important clients.

J. Walter Thompson was also at the forefront of scientific research in the advertising industry. The company used medical and scientific findings in its advertising messages. It also began the now common practice of

*Promoting Life Savers mints in the 1930s with a car decorated in the well-known shape of the product.*

running a consumer panel to survey the buying habits of families and use the results to improve advertising. The company also employed famous academics to study people's motivations for buying and how they responded to different types of advertising.

## Testimonials

Testimonials are glowing letters or quotes from users of a product that become part of an ad. J. Walter Thompson was one of the first ad agencies to use testimonials from famous and respected people, including actress Sarah Bernhardt and Alice Roosevelt, the daughter of U.S. president Theodore Roosevelt.

## New media

As advertising developed in the 20th century, so did technology, and new types of media were invented that could be used to advertise messages. Advertisers quickly seized upon the movies, radio, and television as new and exciting ways to deliver a message. The very first radio commercial, for example, was broadcast on New York's WEAF station in 1922. The ad for a new apartment building cost just $50 to place but resulted in sales totalling thousands. Soon, many companies were buying advertising time on radio or sponsoring entire shows. By the 1930s in the United States, the amount of money spent on radio advertising was more than that spent on magazine advertising. TV advertising become a major advertising medium after World War II, when many homeowners began buying televisions.

## Advertising characters and icons

Throughout the 20th century, some advertisers found great success in using a character to promote their brand or company name. Customers liked a character advertising a brand far more than just a company name or logo. Over time, some of these brand characters have become world-famous. One of the oldest advertising icons is the Michelin Man, a cartoon figure made of tires. It first appeared in 1898 and is still used today to sell Michelin tires in more than 150 countries.

Thirty years after the Michelin Man's debut, a hunchbacked, scowling giant in a bearskin made its first appearance in ads for the Minnesota Valley Canning Company. The ad flopped and was about to be discarded when it received a re-design by the advertising agency Erwin, Wasey & Co. The giant figure was made brighter and more friendly, with a broad smile and an outfit of natural leaves. It was then placed standing over a valley of healthy crops. The Jolly Green Giant was born. The campaign was so successful that in 1950, the Minnesota Valley Canning Company changed its name to Green Giant Co.

## Top brand icons of the 20th century

**Ronald McDonald** – McDonald's restaurants

**The Jolly Green Giant** – Green Giant vegetables

**Betty Crocker** – Betty Crocker food products

**The Energizer Bunny** – Eveready Energizer batteries

**The Pillsbury Doughboy** – Assorted Pillsbury foods

**Aunt Jemima** – Aunt Jemima pancake mixes and syrup

**The Michelin Man** – Michelin tires

**Tony the Tiger** – Kellogg's Frosted Flakes

**Elsie the Cow** – Borden dairy products

Source: *Advertising Age*

# Changing icons

Many brand icons have changed over the years to reflect the changing attitudes of consumers. Kellogg's cartoon tiger, Tony, began life in 1952 looking very much like a real tiger, walking on all four legs. After market research, he became much more humanlike. When people became more health-conscious, Tony reflected this, becoming slimmer and more muscular.

The changes to the Jolly Green Giant were made by a young advertising executive named Leo Burnett, who formed his own company in 1935. Burnett went on to create many of the leading brand characters found in the United States, including the Pillsbury Doughboy and Kellogg's Tony the Tiger.

Today, there are hundreds of brand characters, from the butler on the Ask Jeeves Internet search engine to Ronald McDonald. Characters have even made money for the advertisers from the sale of memorabilia. The "Tetley Tea folk" characters in the United Kingdom and Canada have generated over 200 different collectable items since they first appeared in 1973.

TONY THE TIGER SAYS:

## "You bet your life they're Gr-r-reat!"

No wonder Groucho's speechless. What if a tiger stole your microphone and your favorite line. But that's Tony for you. And he's all for you when he tells you to try these big, crackly flakes of corn. Because they're the ones with the secret Kellogg's sugar coating all over. Gr-r-reat? You bet your life.

*Kellogg's* SUGAR FROSTED FLAKES

*Kellogg's Tony the Tiger went through many image changes. This is what he looked like in the 1950s, appearing with Groucho Marx, host of the* You Bet Your Life *radio show.*

# Running an Advertising Campaign

Some companies produce their advertising campaigns in-house – using their own staff. Most, however, do not have staff with the necessary expertise or experience, and seek out the specialists, the advertising agencies. Advertising can be extremely expensive, so companies think carefully about what they want before contacting ad agencies. They calculate what they can afford, what effects they seek, and who they want to target and how.

*An advertising campaign requires many diverse people to be make it a success. These include management, administration, creative, production, and financial people.*

## Account executive

This person is the main point of contact between the advertiser and the agency. He or she is responsible for communicating the client's wants, questions, likes, and dislikes to the rest of the ad agency team. The account executive must also regularly report to the client and try to resolve disputes quickly and clearly. It can be a tough and stressful job that calls for diplomacy and the ability to negotiate.

An advertising campaign often starts with the advertiser searching for an ad agency. The advertiser may choose to work with an agency it has used in the past, or it may be impressed by the recent work of a rival agency and wish to work with it. Frequently, advertisers may ask several companies to make a pitch for the account. This involves the ad agency giving a presentation suggesting how it would portray the company and its products, what types of channels it may use to reach the right targets, and how much it would cost.

The real work begins for an advertising agency once they have won the account. All advertising agencies are different, but most have separate departments such as research, creative, production, and media. These must all work together to create an advertising campaign. The ad agency starts by obtaining as clear and detailed a plan of what

the advertiser wants as possible. This will include information such as the target audience, the key features the advertiser wishes to communicate about its product or service, and the preferred media used for the advertisement. This information is known as the brief and it may be discussed and updated throughout the life of the campaign's creation.

*Many meetings take place before a company appoints an agency to handle its advertising.*

## THE CAMPAIGN

### briefing

**The client advises the agency of its requirements for an advertising campaign – this is known as the brief.**

The ad agency begins by learning all it can about the product or service to be advertised, its competition, and the target audience. The agency's information department or library collects and reports on surveys and information about the product and the market in which it sells or will sell. For a major advertising campaign, the agency may be instructed to carry out direct research and survey groups of consumers. The goal is to find out what people think about the product area, what attracts them most or turns them away from buying products in this area, and what would encourage them to buy.

## THE CAMPAIGN

### research

**Researchers are sent out to investigate consumers' opinions of the product to identify its strengths and weaknesses.**

## The creative team

In an ad agency, the creation of the actual ads from the brief is the responsibility of the creative team. A creative team consists of copywriters and art directors who work together to come up with concepts, images, and words that will form the core of the campaign. A large advertising agency may have a number of these teams working under a creative director who not only supervises the various teams but may also work directly on very important or high-profile campaigns.

### No secret to success

"There's no secret formula for advertising success, other than to learn everything you can about the product. Most products have some unique characteristic, and the really great advertising comes right out of the product and says something about the product that no one else can say. Or at least no one else is saying."

Advertising executive, Morris Hite, from the book *Adman: Morris Hite's Methods for Winning the Ad Game*, 1988.

## Graphic designer

Graphic designers may work in one or more different media, including print, film, and electronic media, to create designs. They have usually trained at an art school or graphic design college, and have learned to use powerful graphics software running on computer workstations. Some graphic designers specialize in Internet media, in print advertising, in work for TV and film ads, or in the design of logos, signs, and displays.

Copywriters may be asked to come up with one or more short but powerful and effective slogans for the campaign as well as longer pieces of text which form the main text of the ad. For ads in print, on billboards, in newspapers, and in magazines, great importance is placed on the headline and first few words. Copywriters work to produce headlines that will catch readers' interest and attention and propel them into reading the rest of the ad. Some copywriters also work in producing the dialogue, theme, or script of filmed advertisements for television.

At the same time, the art director is working to create the visual ideas of the advertising campaign. With the increased use of computers, many ads involve the manipulation of images and special effects. The final work may be put together by an outside company, but the team led by the art director has to determine in advance what can and cannot be achieved, and plan exactly what they want to see.

THE CAMPAIGN

## 3

## ideas

**A creative team of copywriters and artists begins working on ideas that will form the basis of the campaign.**

# THE CAMPAIGN

## 4

## visuals

**The art director's team prepares initial concepts with storyboards and computer-aided design techniques.**

The art director and graphic designers prepare a layout of the advertisement if it is to be printed. If the advertisement is for television, they prepare storyboards – strip cartoon-like summaries of what the ad will show. If the storyboards and the overall ad are approved, the art director and graphic designers oversee the filming of the commercial, usually by an outside production company. They may also contact talent agencies for suitable actors or models and supervise photo shoots. Throughout the creative process, the team relies on advice and assistance from others in the agency, including the account executive, the production department, and the agency's library or information department.

## Testing times

As a campaign takes shape, there will be rounds of testing on consumers in specially designed focus groups. Approval from the advertiser is also needed. During this period, many changes to campaigns may occur and it can be a stressful time in an agency. But, according to David Ogilvy, the

*Many ideas are considered and rejected before an advertising campaign can proceed. This is all part of the creative process that leads to a successful campaign.*

former head of the giant ad agency Ogilvy & Mather, "The most important word in the vocabulary of advertising is test. If you pre-test your product with consumers, and pre-test your advertising, you will do well in the marketplace." Even when the campaign is completed, a final cycle of testing and approval is usually undertaken. Even more approval must be sought by the media in which the ad is to be shown. Ads must not break the rules or codes of the chosen media, and some ads are returned to the agency that then works with the advertisers to make adjustments.

A large and bewildering array of different media can carry advertising. In the earliest discussions between the advertiser and the agency, in the brief and in later meetings, the exact coverage and frequency of the advertising campaign will be chosen

## THE CAMPAIGN

### 5

### testing

**The first drafts of the campaign are submitted to focus groups whose reactions will determine the next steps.**

and put into action by the media planning and purchasing staff. Campaigns to launch a new product are often burst campaigns. This means that they last for a short time – for example, two or three weeks – but involve ads that appear frequently and in many different channels. Drip campaigns tend to last longer and involve less frequent advertising. These are often used to boost a company's image, or to remind people of a brand's good qualities.

*Testing is one of the most important steps in developing an advertising campaign. Ideas that seem great to those who created them may provoke highly negative reactions from members of the public.*

## Media planner

Media planners gather information on the public's viewing, reading, and Internet habits. They look at and report on the content of different media to help decide which will be most suitable for a particular advertising campaign. Some may also calculate the numbers and types of people reached by different media, and how often they are reached. Media planning calls for expert knowledge of the media available and strong contacts in the industry.

THE CAMPAIGN

### 6

## media

An integral part of campaign planning is deciding which media will do the best job in getting the message across.

*"A great ad campaign will make a bad product fail faster. It will get more people to know it's bad."*

*William Bernbach,
from the book
Bill Bernbach Said
(1989)*

## After the launch

Once the campaign is launched, ad agencies may continue to work with advertisers to try to measure how the campaign is performing. The quality and timing of ads are monitored. Audience figures are measured using the readership numbers or sales of the newspapers or magazines, or the ratings of the TV shows in which the ads appeared. Next-day recall research may take place. This research surveys people about whether they remember an ad, and if so, what they felt about it and the product being advertised. An ad agency may also scour the news media to see if their campaign has attracted additional publicity or comment.

Many campaigns are allowed to run their scheduled course, but if the advertiser is unhappy with the response to the campaign, changes may be made. Some campaigns may do well in testing, but then flop with audiences. Ads may be criticized by pressure groups or advertising watchdog organizations and companies may decide to withdraw a particular ad and replace it with another before they receive more damaging criticism from these groups.

Other things can go wrong in the early life of an advertising campaign. Strikes in the printing or television industry can disrupt a campaign. So can revelations or events surrounding a celebrity used in the campaign. In 2002, 7-Up used the captain of the

# THE CAMPAIGN

## 7

## launch

**When the advertisements are ready and all media are booked, the campaign is launched publicly.**

Irish soccer team, Roy Keane, in its World Cup advertising campaign. Printing his face on cans and billboards, they expected him and their product to get much coverage at the sports event, watched by a total TV audience of more than a billion people.

## Media buyer

Media buyers track the media space and times available, as well as the prices. Senior media buyers negotiate and purchase time and space for ads, and may oversee million-dollar budgets. They also make sure that ads appear exactly as scheduled, such as in the correct edition of a magazine or at the agreed times on radio or television.

your logo here

## Ads in space

Advertising has even reached into space. In 1996, Pepsi paid the Russian space agency to inflate a giant replica of a Pepsi can on board the orbiting space station, Mir. In 2000, Pizza Hut paid an estimated $1 million to have their logo painted onto the side of a Russian rocket carrying an important part of the International Space Station. The launch was watched by an estimated TV audience of more than 450 million.

## Tough but rewarding

"Working in advertising is not as glamorous as many think. The hours can be long, the money not great, especially when you start, and the stress can mount when an advertiser wants changes. But there are plenty of rewards, including working with fascinating, creative people and the pleasure you get on seeing your campaign up there in lights."

Ian Hutchins, account handler at an international agency.

Unfortunately, Keane argued with his team's manager and left before the World Cup started. Another ad campaign, this one for Brylcreem hair products, featured a famous soccer player, David Beckham. The ad campaign flopped after Beckham shaved his head not long after endorsing the product.

Sometimes, the campaigns are simply poorly judged or executed. On other occasions, the product itself may not excite and capture the imagination of the public. "The product that will not sell without advertising will not sell profitably with advertising," said the former head of the Lord & Thomas ad agency, Albert Lasker. The famous American advertising executive, Morris Hite, maintained that "Regardless of how much talent an ad agency may have, it is ineffective without good products and services to advertise."

## Too successful?

Sometimes, advertisers are not ready for the increased demand that an ad campaign can bring. One of the most famous ad campaign "failures" in Great Britain was for Hoover's, an appliance company whose sales promotion offered free flights to the United States for every purchase over $200.

Due to the contest's complicated paperwork and strict deadlines, Hoover had expected few people to pursue the offer. But more than 220,000 consumers bought products and applied, costing the company $95 million and forcing it to sell out to a rival company.

# Advertising Techniques

**M**any different advertising techniques are used to persuade or influence a target audience. Some are straightforward, such as announcements that a store has a sale or that a product or service has just been voted the best in its class by a particular magazine or survey. Others are more subtle and complicated, such as using humor to reinforce a brand or company name while barely mentioning the product.

Many ads place the product or service at the center of the campaign. For example, if a product has a feature or an advantage that rivals lack, this may be highlighted. The advantage or benefit has to be of importance to the target audience for it to persuade them. Common examples of advantage advertising are slogans such as "Half the fat of leading brands," "Twenty percent cheaper," or "Works up to three times as fast." Even if consumers may be aware that several products offer the same advantage or benefit, the advertiser that brings that benefit to mind often gets the sale.

*For the aggressive style of neon advertising, used in shopping and nightlife districts of Hong Kong, many of the signs are suspended over the street on scaffolding.*

Comparative advertising directly compares one company's product with another named company's product – for example, "Our battery lasts twice as long as the Excel Powerbattery." In many European countries, direct comparative advertising is illegal.

*Advertisers do their best to project an ideal world for their products. This can involve tear-jerking moments like the one shown above.*

In the United States, advertisers compare their products, feature by feature, with their competitors. In the United Kingdom, comparative advertising has been allowed since 1994 providing it does "not unfairly attack or discredit other businesses or their products."

Many products are very similar to their rivals. Products such as canned foods, soft drinks, gasoline, and other basic goods may not have a unique selling proposition (USP) that separates them as being radically different than others. When this is the case, advertisers may choose one of a range of techniques to make their product stand out. Repetition and frequency of advertising can be successful techniques, but they cost a large amount, and often only the biggest advertisers can afford them.

*Grandparents in happy moments with grandchildren are another theme used in advertising.*

blah, blah, blah, blah, blah, blah

## Media chatter

Advertisers often hope to create media chatter. This describes getting consumers and the media to talk about the product outside an advertising campaign. A strong slogan or catchphrase that becomes used in everyday life can generate lots of media chatter.

Many advertisers like to associate their products with perfect families, free of conflict or normal day-to-day problems.

Some ads try to generate pressure on the audience to make them choose or act quickly by urging customers to buy now before the offer or stocks of the product run out. Other ads use science to make their product look new and futuristic. Many ads for shampoo and beauty products, for instance, mention their laboratories or feature white lab-coat-wearing actors in their commercials. By contrast, some ads use nostalgia – looking back fondly to the past – to make a product appear classic, timeless, and successful over many decades, even when it has only been invented recently.

## Unique selling proposition – USP

Coined by a famous adman, Rosser Reeves, USP describes any important property of a product or service that makes it different and superior to rival products. Companies seek out a strong USP when developing a new product and often feature it in their launch advertising. Reeves' most famous ad slogan was based on the USP for M&Ms chocolates: "They melt in your mouth, not in your hands."

## Scare and sell

Association can be used in reverse, using something already hated or feared by the target audience. Only the advertised product can solve the problem. These ads are sometimes nicknamed "scare and sell ads."

Humor and human-interest stories are often found in advertising in all the media channels. Sales research shows that humor can help ease people's suspicions toward advertising. Human-interest ads often place the product at the center of a mini-drama with the goal of capturing and keeping interest.

One of the most successful of these mini-dramas was for Gold Blend instant coffee. Over a long series of ads, it portrayed a budding romance between an upper-class couple that was centered around their coffee drinking. The campaign captured the imagination of millions of viewers and sales

rocketed by 40 percent. It also made a star out of the male actor who appeared in the ads, Anthony Stewart Head, who went on to play Giles in the *Buffy the Vampire Slayer* TV series.

## Human dreams, human fears

Although advertising has become more sophisticated over the years, many of the basic techniques exploit ancient human emotions and needs. These include the desire for security, financial success and good health, popularity among friends, high status among co-workers, and sexual attractiveness. Many ads in almost all media channels sell feelings and emotions, stressing the benefits the buyer of the product might enjoy rather than the product itself. An advertisement for a car may not explain the vehicle's features and performance, but instead it may present the car as a way to become more attractive to partners or to improve status at work.

*A favorite technique with advertisers is the use of figures such as scientists (left) and medical personnel (opposite) to present a reassuring image of their products to consumers.*

While many ads show positive images of success, happiness, and health, others appeal to people's guilt, fears, or problems. The guilt is often used by charities and governments in advertising that promotes ideas or that urges people to donate time or money. After making an audience feel guilty, ads show the way that the audience can get rid of that guilt. In a similar way, some ads emphasize problems or fears, such as the fear of crime, of losing your job, or of splitting up with your partner. The product being advertised is pitched as the solution to the fear or problem that has often been exaggerated for effect.

## Prevention, protection, relief

There are three types of ads that prey on people's fears.

*Prevention* ads stress how you can "avoid the bad" – if you are afraid of burglary, you can install an alarm system.

*Protection* ads shows how you can "keep the good" – the good health of your pet can be assured through giving them the right food.

*Relief* ads show the problem or fear already in people, such as stress or too much debt, and offer a solution to "get rid of the bad."

## Association and celebrities

Association is one of the most common and powerful advertising techniques. This is when a product is linked to a desirable person, group, or situation. The goal is to make the product appear as desirable as the things around the subject. For example, an ad for a new car may show it driving through spectacular or beautiful scenery, while an item of clothing may be shown being worn by a glamorous model.

When association is used in TV commercials, it often makes strong use of settings and soundtracks. For instance, food products may use a classical music soundtrack while the images show the food being served to rich people at a luxurious banquet. The goal is to make the audience associate the food with an image of luxury and high quality.

Association works with many different products and target audiences. For example, an ad for a low-priced product may deliberately be made to look cheap and simple, while fashionable and cool settings, soundtracks, and people may be used in ads targeted at fashion-conscious teenagers.

Celebrities have been used to promote products ever since advertising began to boom in the 19th century. They are used in advertising in a variety of ways. They sometimes provide testimonials endorsing the product and claiming that they use, enjoy, or are impressed by it.

Some ads relate directly to the celebrity's job, such as a famous businessman using a particular brand of computer. Most, though, are not directly related. To associate its watches with science, accuracy, and quality, Omega chose celebrities such as former NASA astronaut Thomas Stafford and Grand Prix/Formula One Champion Michael Schumacher.

Top sports stars are often in demand as they convey a message of success, good health, and fitness. Tennis player Venus Williams, for example, signed a $40 million contract to advertise and promote Reebok sportswear.

## Got Milk?

The "Got Milk?" advertising campaign, featuring celebrities with milk mustaches, has been a great success in the United States since its launch in 1996. In 2001 and 2002, the campaign focused on getting teenagers to drink more milk. To appeal to the teenagers, the campaign used "cool" celebrities such as Lara Croft, skateboarding legend Tony Hawk, and hip-hop star Nelly. By 2003, teenagers were drinking nearly 10 percent more milk than previously.

Statistics from the National Family Opinion's Share of Intake Panel (SIP), 2003.

## Shock tactics

Shock advertising uses a particularly surprising or disturbing image or message to grab attention and make a persuasive and memorable point. The perils of drinking alcohol and driving, and the dangers of HIV/AIDs, are two areas where shock advertising has been used by governments of many countries.

Shock advertising has been heavily criticized since it upsets people. It is still in use. Charities use it to highlight the plight of people or animals in need of help. In 2003, the children's charity Barnardo's used a computer-generated photo of a newborn baby with a cockroach crawling out of its mouth to highlight child poverty. Complaints caused the ad to be withdrawn. However, the publicity the campaign received made the ad widely admired by the UK advertising industry.

*Champion tennis player Venus Williams, who signed a $40 million promotional contract with Reebok.*

# Advertising & You

Advertising is a powerful tool of persuasion and influence, but it does have its critics. Most of the criticism can be divided into two areas: the effect on business and prices, and the impact on people in society. Critics argue that advertising adds large amounts to the cost of many products, does not always bring results, and is seen by some as wasteful and unnecessary. More than 100 years ago, department store owner John Wanamaker (of Wanamaker's Department Stores in Philadelphia and New York) lamented, "I know I waste half the money I spend on advertising. The problem is, I don't know which half."

Many critics argue that advertising also helps restrict new competition by creating a barrier to entry. To enter a market selling detergent or soft drinks, a new company needs an advertising budget of many millions in order to simply match existing advertisers.

"Advertising makes people discontented. It makes them want things they don't have."

Ray Locke, former owner of ad agency Tracy-Locke Co. (quoted by Department of Advertising, University of Texas)

## Motivations

"Our children would find it a lot easier to make healthy food choices if advertising wasn't pulling them in the opposite direction."

Kaye Mehta, chairwoman of the Coalition on Food Advertising to Children (quoted in *The Age*, February 24, 2004)

Some people and campaign groups fear that advertising creates problems for people in society. Advertising, they argue, encourages greed and an obsession with buying and consuming more and more products, and this leads to waste. It uses subtle and powerful messages to promote ways of living beyond the reach of most people. This can lead to frustration, unhappiness, debt, and even sickness.

## Justifications

"The more fully consumers are informed, the better equipped they will be to make purchase decisions appropriate to their own needs. Advertising is a principal means by which useful information is delivered to consumers."

Mary L. Azcuenaga, Commissioner of the Federal Trade Commission, from a speech entitled "Advertising Regulation and the Free Market" made at the International Congress of Advertising and Free Market, Lima, Peru, 1995.

## Investigate advertising messages

Examine ads from a variety of channels and see if they use any of the following common appeals or messages.

### Join the club

Everyone else is using the product, you do not want be left out.

### Be elite

Using a product makes you part of a glamorous group.

### Be patriotic

Using a product shows a love of and pride in your country.

### Stand out

Owning or using the product puts you ahead of the pack and makes you different and better than everyone else.

### Promote your sex appeal

Doing what the ad suggests will make you more attractive to others.

### We address your hidden fears

A bad situation will or may occur if you do not follow the ad's suggestion.

For example, the use of beautiful, thin female models in much advertising is claimed to contribute to the large number of teenage girls and young women with eating disorders. Many groups are especially concerned about advertising for toys, clothes, and fast food targeted at children. In Australia, the Coalition on Food Advertising to Children (CFAC) is fighting to outlaw all food ads shown during children's viewing hours because they claim there is a link between these ads and the country's 1.5 million overweight children.

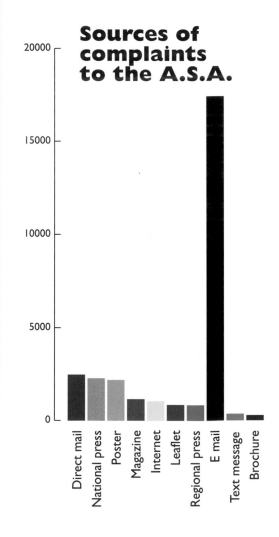

### Sources of complaints to the A.S.A.

## Advertising and the individual

Many people feel that they are completely powerless in the face of the mass of advertising that surrounds them. This does not have to be the case. First, people can become more critical consumers. This does not mean they must become anti-advertising. It means that they can learn more about the process of advertising and learn and understand many of the ways it gets messages across. People should not simply accept an advertiser's claims. Before buying, they should seek out other views of the product or service, such as independent reviews in magazines on the Internet.

Second, if people find a particular ad or campaign makes false or misleading claims or offends and upsets, they have the right to complain to the advertiser, the advertising agency, or the media channel on which the ad was placed. Newspapers, TV networks, and radio stations regularly receive and investigate complaints and, in some cases, remove ads.

*People often find advertising offensive or believe it is misleading. Most do not lodge formal complaints, but simply penalize the product by not buying it. Others take positive action, complaining to relevant industry bodies or official organizations.*

## American Advertising Federation Code key principles

Advertising shall tell the truth and any claims should be based on fact. It should also reveal important facts which would mislead the public if not told.

Advertising should not make false or misleading claims about a rival or their products or services.

Advertising shall be free of statements, illustrations, or implications that are offensive to good taste or public decency.

Advertising shall avoid price claims that are false or misleading, or saving claims that do not offer provable savings.

Advertising containing testimonials shall be limited to those of competent witnesses who are reflecting a real and honest opinion or experience.

## Toy-makers' tricks

*Rules and codes on advertising to children say that the ad should show toys in a realistic way, but some advertisers use the following tricks in their ads:*

*Cut out the boring parts of playing with the toy, such as putting it together.*

*Show the toy alongside many others that must be bought separately.*

*Use trick camera angles to make a toy look bigger or faster-moving than it really is.*

*Place the toy in an exciting fantasy world that is more exciting than the toy in real life.*

In 2000, an ad for Nike ACG Air Dri-Goat running shoes was pulled from a number of U.S. outdoor and sports magazines after complaints that its copy labeled people with disabilities as "drooling and misshapen." The company apologized in print and on their website.

The advertising industries of most countries regulate most of their own activities and have codes of practice in place that advertisers must observe. Advertising watchdogs are organizations that uphold these codes and are designed to protect people from advertising that is offensive, illegal, false, or misleading. In the United States, the American Advertising Federation, the National Advertising Review Council (NARC), and the Children's Advertising Review Unit are all industry-run watchdogs.

*Patriotism and the creation of wealth are two of the favorite incentives used by advertisers around the world.*

## Complaints to the A.S.A., 2003

| | |
|---|---|
| **14,277** | complaints received |
| **10,754** | advertisements complained about |
| **1,613** | investigations |
| **1,702** | non-broadcast ads were changed or withdrawn |
| **4,717** | complaints about honesty and truth |
| **3,707** | complaints about taste and decency |

In addition, an arm of the U.S. government, the Federal Trade Commission, has powers to halt advertising that is false or deceives people. They can also make advertisers place certain information in future advertisements to right the wrongs in their previous ads.

In the United Kingdom, Ofcom is the watchdog for television, radio, and telecommunications, and the Advertising Standards Authority (ASA) investigates public complaints about ads in other channels such as direct mail and print ads in newspapers. In a country of over 59 million people, it can take less than 100 complaints for an ad to be investigated by the ASA. While many ads are cleared of wrongdoing, a number of complaints are upheld. This usually leads to the ads being withdrawn and, in some cases, public apologies given.

Occasionally, the work or campaigns of advertisers and their ad agencies may break laws in a country and result in more than just an ad being banned. In 1991, the car-makers Volvo and their ad agency, Scali McCabe Sloves, were found guilty of rigging an advertisement showing a Volvo and rivals' cars being hit by a pick-up truck. The rivals' cars had been deliberately weakened beforehand and the Volvo strengthened with reinforced steel. This gave the false impression that the Volvo car was much stronger than other models. The two companies were fined $150,000. Some advertising critics believe that such penalties should be in place all the time to prevent advertisers and their ad agencies from exaggerating or deceiving.

## Acne ads

In 2003, an ad for Zapzyt Acne Treatment Gel was aired on U.S. TV in the middle of children's shows. The Children's Advertising Review Unit's guidelines state that "Medications and drugs should not be advertised to children." The ad was never played again during children's TV shows.

**brand name**
distinctive name by which a particular product or a group of products is known

**B2B (Business to Business) advertising**
advertising aimed at companies, rather than at the consumer

**campaign**
total planned advertising effort on behalf of a specific client or product

**channel**
type of media through which an advertising message can be best presented

**classified ad**
brief listing appearing in a newspaper or magazine that offers products or services for sale, or a small advertising announcement

**client**
organization that employs an advertising agency to create advertisements

**commercial**
audio or video advertising announcement, usually shown on television or radio

**concept**
general idea behind a slogan or campaign

**consumer**
person who buys, or whom advertisers decide should buy, advertised products and services

**copy**
written part of an advertisement

**direct mail**
advertising sent to people's homes

**focus group**
group of potential consumers who are quizzed about opinions on a product, a concept, or an advertising campaign

**logo**
mark, word, or symbol that represents a company or product

**market research**
investigations into consumers, their buying habits, and how goods and services reach them

**market share**
percentage of a market held by a particular brand or company

**media**
types of mass communication carrying advertising, including newspapers, magazines, direct mail, billboards, bus signs, radio, television, the Internet

**press**
newspapers, magazines, and journals for both consumer and business readers

**pressure group**
group of people who try actively to influence governments, change laws, or influence the public on an issue

**product placement**
form of advertising in which companies pay to place their products in a regular

TV show, radio show, or movie

**storyboard**
series of panels roughly depicting scenes, copy, and shots proposed for a television commercial

**target audience**
consumer group most likely to buy a specific product or service, usually identified by age, region, and income

**testimonial**
statement, often given by a celebrity, confirming the value of a product, event, or service

**test market**
consumer group interviewed to determine target audience

**tie-in**
campaign to link products, media, or markets

**unique selling proposition (USP)**
characteristic that makes a product different from another product

**voice-over (VO)**
recorded off-screen voice heard on a television or radio advertisement

## Books

Higgins, Denis, ed., *The Art of Writing Advertising: Conversations with William Bernbach, Leo Burnett, George Gribbin, David Ogilvy, Rosser Reeves*. New York: NTC Business Books, 1986.

Ogilvy, David, *Confessions of an Advertising Man*. New York: Atheneum, 1988.

Ogilvy, David, *Ogilvy on Advertising*. New York: Vintage, 1985.

Oller, John W. and J. Roland Giardetti. *Images that Work: Creating Successful Messages in Marketing and High Stakes Communication*. Westport, Conn.: Quorum, 1999.

Packard, Vance. *The Hidden Persuaders*. New York: Random House, 1957.

# Organizations

**American Advertising Federation**
1101 Vermont Avenue, NW
Suite 500
Washington, D.C. 20005

**Children's Advertising Review Unit**
70 West 36th Street, 13th Floor
New York, N.Y. 10018

**Federal Trade Commission**
600 Pennsylvania Avenue, NW
Washington, D.C. 20580

**National Advertising Review Council**
70 West 36th Street, 13th Floor
New York, N.Y. 10018